Author's Biography

The Supreme Master Ching Hai was born in Central Au Lac (Vietnam). At the age of eighteen, Master Ching Hai moved to England to study, and then later to France and then Germany, where She worked for the Red Cross and married a German physician. After two years of happy marriage, with Her husband's blessings, She left Her marriage in pursuit of enlightenment, thus fulfilling an ideal that had been with Her since Her childhood.

This began a time of arduous pilgrimages to many different countries that ended only when She met a perfect living Master in the Himalayas. Master Ching Hai received the divine transmission of the inner Light and Sound, which She later called the Quan Yin Method. After a period of diligent practice, She attained Perfect Enlightenment. To satisfy the longing of sincere Truth seekers, the Supreme Master Ching Hai offers the Quan Yin Method of meditation to people of all nationalities, religions and cultural backgrounds. Her message of love and peace brings spiritual liberation and hope to people throughout the world, reminding all to uphold Truth, Virtue, and Beauty in life.

Love is The Only Solution

"Love is the greatest thing in life and the greatest thing in the entire universe. But most people nowadays are lacking that love. Humanity must show more love than before. We must love even our enemies, our neighbors, animals and the environment around us, then we can overcome the crisis and have a peaceful life. Love must be manifested outwardly. Love can't be talked about, but must be shown through action. That is, to be vegan, do good and protect the environment."[1]

"I need the demonstration of love, just 1% more love for the world, love for your children, love for all species, enough so that we will sacrifice our taste for the animals' meat, and related unmerciful products. We have to show love in a grander scale, not just romantic love for our family members – we should keep that, because every kind of love is sacred. Every kind of love will emit some beautiful positive energy to protect us, and to protect loved ones and something around us.

So if each one of us gives more love into the surroundings, extends it, like more, a little bit further than family, and enough of that love, that will make up for the 100% love power needed to dissolve the greatest threat to our survival."[2]

-Supreme Master Ching Hai

1

The Current
Global Situation

was thinking, "How come the world is not better yet?" I mean, not the way I want. Not like completely better. Not like Heaven and peace for everybody. Still, it's very chaotic at the moment. Not the pandemic only, but the animals die by the hundreds of thousands because they cannot sell. They kill them, hundreds of thousands. Pigs or cows or chickens, minks. And then the whole world is in deficit. Because of the pandemic, people don't work, they're less productive, but more payment. Even I heard Americans' debt is like some US$30 trillion, something like that. Some trillions anyway.

And then there is Ebola. But it's probably better now. And the salmonella in chickens, etc., etc. And the seasonal flu has still not disappeared ever. Visits us again and again, and that's also sometimes deadly, or very uncomfortable and very damaging to the body. Because if you take antibiotics, it's also not good for the body. And then even those sicknesses before, like SARS and MERS and stuff like that, they're still in the corner, somewhere. Maybe they don't spread so quickly like COVID-19 but they are still spreading.

It's just because the COVID-19 now covers everything.
Many cancer patients are neglected. People complained,
and the newspaper printed them. And Tuberculosis is
neglected. And malaria, people with other kinds of chronic
disease or dangerous disease, many are neglected because of
the COVID-19 situation. Lockdown, and hospitals are full, and
the pandemic is new and more urgent. So, many patients
are not really cared for, and die. Especially the elderly.

So it's not only the pandemic that kills people, there are
other things as well. Other old epidemics/pandemics are
also still ongoing. And now we have even floods, torrential
rains and landslides in many places, and the locust disaster

in many places, bee declines, also droughts everywhere, and farmers – helpless; no one can help them. It's worrisome for our world, some people worry that due to all this, we will have food shortage.

And even mental stress. Even some doctors killed themselves, because of the situation and maybe the virus attacked their brain, so they could not even think straight. That's what it was. I saw one doctor, so beautiful, American, just killed herself like that. And many more. And many doctors and hospital personnel and nurses died because of infection. Because in the beginning nobody prepared for this, so they didn't have enough equipment for protection, so they just died like that. Imagine, these heroic people.

And then in England, like doctors and nurses already retired, they came back out again. Just to help out because they are needed. The hospitals called them, and they came back and sacrificed, and they died. Many of them. Just like that! Imagine. Yeah, terrible! How would you feel if you are their family members? Normally they work hard all their lives already. And then, now they enjoy a little bit of leftover of their time on Earth, they have to sacrifice and die just like that! I feel it's not fair.[3]

It's a big cleaning time. And even if we get over this, others will come. And nowadays, we have so many things coming, not just this. We have Ebola and we have salmonella from the chicken farms and all that stuff. And even the minks, you know the minks that people peel the fur to wear? Like in some European country, I think it was, Holland, they killed thousands and thousands of them, because they're afraid of the transmission of the disease. But no matter how many animals you kill, it doesn't help if you don't change your way of life.

If you keep cutting the forest and let the wild have nowhere to live, and then we get closer and closer to the wild animals, then they will transmit the disease in any way. And then one jumps to another, and then the world is in trouble like this. We just have to leave the animals in peace if we want peace. That's it. That's very simple. More I cannot say. More I cannot say because that is the fact and everybody knows it.[4]

2 The Environment

I'm sure many of you are aware of the increasing number of global warming effects noted worldwide, so I will share just a few from the world and from the United States.

In the Arctic, North Pole, so much ice has already melted that scientists are forecasting an ice-free summer within as little as three to six years, which would be the first time in one million years! Meanwhile, Greenland is shedding 85 million tons of icebergs each day due to warming, and at a rate that is increasing by 7% each year. The West Antarctic Ice Shelf is also melting, with 3.3 meter sea level rises forecast that would threaten cities like in your country, New York, Washington, D.C., and San Francisco. And if all of Antarctica and Greenland were to melt – meaning the ice – then the sea levels could rise to as much as 70 meters, which would be deadly or disastrous to most lives on Earth.

Glaciers across the globe are shrinking more quickly than researchers ever expected, leaving rivers and lakes gone, disappearing or drying, with no water for crops and billions who face food shortages due to water shortages, as well. Due to rising sea levels, islands are sinking as we speak, with Tuvalu, Tonga and some 40 other island nations having to plan their whole country's migrations.

Love Is The Only Solution

They are being forced to join the already 20 million climate refugees today. The International Organization for Migration stated that there may be 200 million climate refugees by 2050.

According to researchers at Georgia Institute of Technology, United States of America, worldwide the number of the most destructive Category 4 and 5 hurricanes has doubled over the past 35 years. Category 5 storms yield the highest level of destruction in major cities. Their intensity and duration have also increased by 75% since the 1970s. One of these storms whose effects can still be seen and felt was the 2005 Hurricane Katrina, which devastated, especially, areas of New Orleans, with people who are still recovering their homes and their lives today. I am so sorry the American people have had to suffer through such tragedies.

Now, in the United States: Close to a million acres of pine forest have been lost in the Rocky Mountains due to beetle infestation from global warming. Similar also in Canada but, due to the time limit, I cannot report to you everything, so now we just report about the United States.

kinds of diseases, which inflict suffering on our world. So some people with little faith blame God again. Wherever I gave lectures, people would ask me, "If there is a God, why has such and such disaster happened?" But these people should remember that it's not God who does all these things; it's we who make all these troubles. For example, a few nations always test atom bombs and hydrogen bombs, which disturbs the construction of the atmosphere and then shake the stability of the Earth. They think that just shooting the bombs into the air or into the ocean won't make any problems. But this still creates problems because the universe is constructed with many kinds of materials; some with solid substances and some with invisible substances. So by disturbing the invisible substances they also disturb the stability of the universe and interfere with the revolution of nature.

For example, you build a house with windows, doors and some empty rooms. If one of the corners is broken, then the temperature in the room will change. Even though it is the summer, at night, it will be very cold if the broken hole is not mended, because sometimes in the night, cold wind and rain will come.[6]

Protect Our Heroic Compassionate Self

We must save the human and human compassionate heart – that is the most important. We have to save our noble quality. Again and again, I always mention, it's not just about the physical existence on this planet that we want to save, but we want to protect the children, and by doing that we protect our noble Self, our heroic compassionate Self, which is our true Nature. If we lose them, it's worse than losing the planet. We have to keep our compassionate heart.

We have to be noble and truthful, loving and protective of the weak and the feeble, like children and the helpless defenseless animals. We must protect our noble Nature, we must be living, walking, breathing children of God, or the disciples of the Buddhas.[7]

Love Begets Love

Because first of all, we have to practice love in order to beget love. In order to be all-pervasive, loving, like our Father, we have to love all beings. And that is the meaning behind the vegan diet. It's not to be healthy, or not because Jesus said so or Buddha forbids, it's just we have to be love reincarnate.

We have to be the walking God on this planet. We have to live like God would live, in order to be near God... God doesn't punish us, it's just like begets like. If we want to be near to something, we have to go there, the same direction. So, God created all beings and let them die naturally. So should we. If we couldn't create, at least we do not destroy. The commandment in the Bible is: "Thou shall not kill." It didn't say: "You shall not kill humans only." It says, "Thou shall not kill." Anything killed is killed.[8]

4 The Answer to all of Humanity's Problems is LOVE

Love is the most precious thing in this physical realm. So we must protect love, be it the love between a couple, between parents and children, between friends. Love between humans or love between animals, love between humans and animals or between animals and humans. Be it even the love between plants and trees. They do communicate. They do love and protect each other, as scientists have proven. You read about them, you know. Real love is what we need to protect our world, especially now. Whatever we love will blossom. Whatever loves us makes us grow in happiness. But love is not just a vocabulary; love is action, invisible and visible.

Love Is The Only Solution

Love can flourish or be destroyed even, though the essence of love can never be destroyed. There are deeds that can nourish love, there are deeds that can make love wither and die. I mean physical love. I mean the love in this realm. There are deeds that can make love grow, there are deeds that can make love diminish. We must cherish, treasure love if we find it. Support it. We have to support it with our thoughts and speech and actions.[2]

We can be and should be the example of love, like giving, caring, and harmonizing, so that when others think of us, remember our names, they would feel happiness, love, comfort, and even noble. And their good quality will shine forth. We should not be the source of burden or misery to others, in their thoughts, deeds, and speech.

We have to be the source of inspiration, of nobility and love, especially if we have been shown how, by others' example. If we have love, all good will come our way. We can start to love now, today, and continue tomorrow into the future. ***Love yourself, love your family, love your neighbors, love all around us.***

Without love in our heart, we are almost nothing, just a burden to ourselves, to loved ones, and society. Love is not a word on our lips, love must be our feeling inside, and action translated outside.

Love the animals, we'll be vegan.

Love the Earth, we'll go green.

Love the world, save the planet.[2]

If we consider ourselves higher beings, then we should carry out higher noble acts – protect the weak and the innocent, and not abuse our power by harming our friends, especially since they do us no harm. We should listen to the great wise religious leaders of the past and present, and regard our animal friends as sacred, cherished creations of God. And as a very basic gesture of dignity, respect and kindness, we should be vegan. When we love and respect the animals, we will develop our own spirituality.

When we are able to expand this love to all other beings of the universe, including the animals who are our co- inhabitants, we ourselves expand and become greater spiritually. A peaceful relationship with the animals, with no more killing, would attract to us an abundance of Divine blessings. And with the whole world extending such compassion to animals our planet's atmosphere, of course, would stabilize and even change to a more heavenly-like, permeated with feelings of peace and love.[9]

If we are in the organic vegan trend or planting organic vegan farming method, then you will feel more and more the love from nature, the love from the planet Earth, the love from the trees, the love from even a blade of grass, from flowers. We will feel so much love in the air that we breathe. We feel so much love from the earth that we walk on. This we cannot even explain in human language. We must feel it. I always feel it, but I can't transmit this spiritual message to other people. Everyone must experience it for himself. Once we turn to a compassionate Heaven intended lifestyle of a vegan diet, then we will feel more and more love, more and more connected all the time.[10]

First, be vegan, okay? If we can't find the organic vegetables or fruits, then please, be vegan first. Because this positive loving energy will envelop our planet, will be a protective shield for us. There's nothing else, no other green power can protect us in this crucial moment

of danger. Please believe me. I have nothing to gain from telling you this, but I tell you because I'm one of you, because my love doesn't know any boundary between me, myself, my family or my country people or the people of Korea, or any other nationalities in the world. I love all people. I love all the beings on this planet and I want to save you all. I want to save them all. Please wake up and wake everybody else up before our house is burned down. Together we will win, together we will save this planet. Not to save the planet for the sake of material existence, but because we save ourselves.

We save our great Self which is compassionate, which is loving, which is merciful, which is godlike. All the scriptures of the religions tell us this, that we are the Buddha, that we can become Buddha as soon as we want, that we are the children of God. So we have to save our status as the greatest beings in the universe; the crown of the creation. We must save our great quality; not just the planet, but ourselves, our heart, our nobility, our leadership on this beautiful spaceship we call planet Earth. We are the captains. We must lead the planet into safety and save our soul, save the best qualities that we have within us.

Together, we can maintain not only the beautiful Jeju and all the South Korea as a wonderful paradise, but we will also save the whole world. You will all become heroes. You will all be my heroes. Please, be veg, go green. Love can change the world. Thank you.[10]

A Message from the Animals

They (the animals) wish the human race can see what they see, know what they know and stop all this madness centering around temporary time on Earth and focus more

on life eternal. They wish the Earth be saved. But it's
not about saving the planet, but about the human
returning to a virtuous life and compassionate heart.
And all things will be all right. They know that. Then
the Earth will be saved if people are compassionate as
a byproduct. If we live according to the law of love, all
things will be all right. The animals know that, and they
would really wish humans understand this concept, the
only concept that matters, the concept of love.[11]

Because after we practice for some time we will feel the
one, at oneness of all things, of ten thousands things
in the universe, the oneness between you and me, of
yourself and myself. That we are from the same source,
we are of wisdom, of love and of oneness. Therefore
he cannot just pick out one person or one being in the
universe and say "I love that person". Right!

If this is the whole from the forehead to the toe is your
body. We will pick one particular and take care of that
toe or thumb? This is my beloved. Can we do that? No,
it would be ridiculous. We might say, we might say, oh,

my lips is beautiful, yeah. I am proud of my hair or I love my thumb, maybe. But we equally love other parts of the body. Because without each part of our body, we cannot live. We will not be able to exist happily, if we cut, cut them or damage one, one part of our body. We will get hurt, we will feel very very hurt, if we are still in sensitive feeling. Only those who are numb or probably have trouble, do not feel when they touch fire or damage part of their body.

The ordinary sensitive human beings feel any trouble in each part of their body. Therefore, the sage is the very ordinary human being, is a true great human being. Because he feels for all things. That's why we do not harm other sentient beings. That's why we become vegan to nourish ourselves, nourish our love for all beings. Because they are all one with us. If we want to ever attain the wholeness of our real self, then we should take care of all beings, because they each one are part of ourselves. That's the reason. Not because the precepts say, say so. It's because of our sensitive feeling.

The more we practice oneness with the heaven and earth, the more we become sensitive to the feeling of every sentient being in the universe. And we automatically try to preserve them. Of course in some cases when it absolutely cannot avoid. Then we might choose the less, the least troublesome, the least harming, like we eat vegan. We would rather not eat but we just have to.[12]

A vegan diet is nonviolence in the highest sense, and a vegan diet is love in action. Don't you think? Yes, if you love animals, why eat them? Yes, everybody says we love animals, but how? And a vegan diet will stop 80% of global warming, stop all the cruelty, beginning on our plate, generating loving, kind energy around the world, stop water shortage and water pollution, stop food shortages, stop world hunger and war, prevent deadly diseases, save enormous tax and medical bills to build a better world and support new useful inventions and good people's organizations, the list goes on and on.

We all want to have a peaceful world and we all talk about how we want peace and love. Well, I think we should start it now and let peace begin on our plates. Let love begin with our choice. All the benefits of vegan diet cannot be overstated. And now there is spiritual aspect also. When a person partakes in direct or indirect killing of any sentient beings, be it human or animals, he or she enters the cycle of revenge and violence. And it will only end when one stops doing it.

Love Is The Only Solution

Hence, we have to love our enemy. Because only love and forgiveness will have the power to break the negative effect of hatred and vengeance. But all Masters and enlightened Saints in the past have already talked about it.[13]

I wish the world vegan. World peace. That's all I wish. Every day I keep repeating that to Heavens, make sure They hear me. To help us. Because without World Vegan, there will not be lasting World Peace. That's why I ask people to pray and meditate only for World Vegan. And World Peace also comes along. The more World Vegan now, the more World Peace. But it should be more lasting. Well, it's much better now, but still, it's not as ideal as I want it. People are more vegan now. They have more time now during COVID-19. They will sit together or they sit alone, with their family, close family, or alone and with one or two, and they have more time to reflect. And we see the vegan trend is getting more prominent now. I wish it will affect the whole world, and then soon we will have no more suffering animals on our planet, or suffering people from war and famine and all that.

I would advise all the leaders to save all the money unnecessary, for war, for other things that are frivolous spending. Keep their money and just give money to the poor. Give them something to start their lives with business, with education, or with farming, with changing their lives about from meat business to organic vegan business. It's very easy. And then they would take care of themselves. And the more people are vegan, the less government leaders should worry, because they will not be so violent if they have enough work for them to do, to earn their money, to take care of themselves; they would never make any trouble for governments. There will be less suffering, then also less sickness and less criminals in the world. Then it's good for everybody.

That's what I wish: World Vegan, World Peace, in the name of God. In God's mercy, may it come soon. Amen.[14]

5 Meditation for Inner and World Peace

Peace begins with us, with me, with you, and then peace will be in the whole world. Therefore, if we meditate, and we omit our intake of meat, then we'll become more peaceful within ourselves. And because we are more peaceful, we will radiate a kind of invisible, peaceful atmosphere around us, which affects everybody. And we do not talk about peace, peace will be. We don't have to advocate peace, peace will be.[15]

Meditation is very popular now. They don't say 'meditate to find God,' but 'meditate to relax, to become healthier, feel better, live longer and be successful.' That is, to be successful in every aspect, we must choose a time during the day to rest, not to sleep, but to meditate. Everyone knows about it now because science has proven it. If we choose a time during the day to rest or meditate, our bodies become healthier. One of the best methods is meditation; that is, choosing a time to meditate every day.

It's a time for you to treasure. We've worked all day, busily taking care of the world and others. So whenever we meditate, that's a time for us. We must love ourselves first — love others but also love ourselves.

It's very good for you. The most precious time for you since the moment you were born and until you die is meditation time. It's the best thing you do for yourselves. No one can give it to you; only you can give it to yourselves. It's the best thing that you can do for yourselves — meditation. While you do it for yourselves, others will naturally benefit as well. Your family, relatives, dogs and cats will also benefit. Trees and flowers will benefit too.[16]

Because really meditation is your shield. That's when you're connected more with your own greater power and the universal force that upholds you, holds you tight and protects you, embraces you with all love and blessing and protection. Truly like that. There's no other power that can protect you in this world. That's the secret. That is the

secret of the universe that not many people understand or
have the privilege to know, but sometimes people take it
for granted and they have trouble and they have sickness
and all that, and they go out and have medicine and then
thank the doctor. It's fine when you're not spiritually strong
enough and the karma overwhelms you, then you have
to go to the doctor. But we have the cure within. And we
can be always healthy and strong to help ourselves and to
shoulder the world, until people are more awakened and
help chip in.[17]

Our Purpose on Earth

"Each one of us is given human life only for the purpose
of realizing God. If we forsake this duty, we will never be
happy in this life or in any other life. To tell you the truth,
this is the only reason for human suffering, and nothing
else. If we realized how we struggled in our mother's
womb, how we repented our past lives' mistakes, and
how we promised God to utilize this present life in a
very meaningful manner to serve Hirm, before we were
born, then we would never waste one second to think of
anything else but to try our best in all our leisure time to
realize God!

But as soon as we are born into this world, we forget
everything. Because it is the law of the material world
to let people forget. Therefore, it is necessary that a
Master come and remind us again, again and again, until
we remember what we had promised to God, inside the
womb of our mother. We might not remember with our
physical brains, but our souls, the ability of our wisdom
will remember."[18]

Meditation: How to Remember Our True Nature

"Every time you pay full attention, one-pointedly and
wholeheartedly, to one thing, that is meditation. Now, I
pay only attention to the inner Power, to the compassion,
to the love, to the mercy quality of God, and that is
meditation. To do so officially, we should just sit in a
quiet corner and be by ourselves, that is the process of
meditation. But it isn't by sitting quietly in a corner that
one gets something. You have to be in contact with that
inner Power first and meditate using that inner Power. This
is called Self awakening. We must awaken the real Self
inside and let Hirm meditate, not our human brain and our
mortal understanding. If not, you will sit down and think

about a thousand things and won't be able to subdue your passions. But when you are self-awakened, the real inner Self, the God power within you, will control everything. You only know real meditation after you are awakened by transmission by a real Master. Otherwise, it is only a waste of time wrestling with your body and mind."

What is the Master and why do we need one?

"A Master is one who has the key for you to become a Master...to help you realize that you are also a Master and that you and God are also One. That's all...that's the only role of the Master."

"Masters are those who remember their Origin and, out of love, share this knowledge with whomever seeks it, and take no pay for their work. They offer all their time, finance and energy to the world. When we reach this level of mastership, not only do we know our Origin, but we can also help others to know their true worth. Those who follow the direction of a Master, quickly find themselves in a new world, full of true knowledge, true beauty and true virtues."

Initiation

"Initiation means the beginning of a new life into a new order. It means that the Master has accepted you to become one of the beings in the circle of Saints. Then, you are no longer an ordinary being, you are elevated, just like when you enroll for university, you are no longer a high school student. In the old times, they called it baptism or taking refuge in the Master.

Initiation actually is just a word for opening the spirit. You see, we are crowded with many kinds of obstacles, invisible as well as visible, so the so-called initiation is the process of opening the gate of wisdom and letting it flow through this world, to bless the world, as well as the so-called Self. But the true Self is always in glory and wisdom, so there is no need of blessing for that."

The Quan Yin method - meditation on Inner Light and Inner Sound

The Inner Light, the Light of God, is the same Light referred to in the word "enlightenment". The Inner Sound, is the Word referred in Bible:" In the beginning was the Word, and the Word was God." It is through the inner Light and Sound that we come to know God.

"So now, if we somehow can get in touch with this Word or Sound Stream, then we can know God's whereabouts, or we can be in contact with God. But what is the proof that we are in contact with this Word? After we are in contact with this inner Vibration, our life changes for the better. We know many things we never knew before. We

understand many things we never thought of before. We can do, accomplish many things we never dreamed of before. We are getting mightier, and mightier. Our being becomes more capable and more enlarged until we are everywhere, until we become omnipresent, and then we know that we became one with God."

The Five Precepts

Supreme Master Ching Hai accepts people from all backgrounds and religious affiliations for initiation. You do not have to change your present religion or system of beliefs. You will not be asked to join any organization, or participate in any way that does not suit your current lifestyle. However, you will be asked to become vegan. A lifetime commitment to the vegan diet is a necessary prerequisite for receiving initiation.

The initiation is offered free of charge. Daily practice of the Quan Yin Method of meditation, and the keeping of the Five Precepts are your only requirements after initiation. The Precepts are guidelines that help you to neither harm yourself nor any other living being.

Refrain from taking the life of sentient beings. This precept requires strict adherence to a vegan diet. No meat, fish, poultry, dairy or eggs.

Refrain from speaking what is not true.

Refrain from taking what is not yours.

Refrain from sexual misconduct.

Refrain from using intoxicants. This includes avoiding all poisons of any kind, such as alcohol, drugs, tobacco, gambling, pornography, and excessively violent films or literature.

* This also includes 2.5 hours per day of meditation on the inner Light and Sound.

These practices will deepen and strengthen your initial enlightenment experience, and allow you to eventually attain the highest levels of Awakening or Buddhahood for yourself. Without daily practice, you will almost certainly forget your enlightenment and return to the lower level of consciousness.[18]

We can always regain all this divinity. Truly, I promise you with all honesty and honor, that we can have it. Every one of you sitting there, whatever age you are, if you don't even have any experience about Heaven, you don't even have any talent before, you don't even know what to meditate on – any one of you can attain this divinity again, reclaim it again, provided we have the right counteraction.

And the first step is to switch to a more compassionate lifestyle, because that is what we are: we are compassion. A compassionate, vegan diet is the basic way of a higher being, a mark of a true human being. A true human being would never kill. A true being would never harm another, even if his own life is threatened. A real gentleman steps wisely, understanding that all beings are connected, and that by taking a life, compromises his own human spirit and bringing the bad retribution of killing upon him.

So, it is not solely the responsibility of these children to improve the world's consciousness level – we must all work together to bring Heaven closer to Earth. We can all do it; it's so simple. In my group, even children 5-6 years old can meditate and can hear the inside melody, can talk to God. If we want to bring Heaven to Earth, if that is our wish, so shall it be.[19]

How to Contact Us

If you are interested in finding out more about receiving initiation from the Supreme Master Ching Hai into the Quan Yin method, please contact one of our Meditation Centers near you from the following list.

www.GodsDirectContact.org.tw/eng/cp/index.htm

6 Supreme Master Ching Hai's Appeal to All Religious and Spiritual Leaders

Your Reverend Holinesses, Highly Reverend Priests, Priestesses, Monks, Nuns of different faiths, my best wishes and humble prayers for Your wellness in God's mercy. Though my time is tight and precious, as I am still in intensive meditation retreat for World Vegan, World Peace, but the urgent call of the planet and our world push me. I feel I must deliver some urgent messages to Your Holinesses and Reverends. As great spiritual leaders, You would also be aware of the devastation occurring on our planet, directly related to accelerated climate change caused by humans' cruel behaviors and brutal habits, which is not so difficult to change once applying the

principle of love. Please tell Your believers this truth. Tell them that we must change. Because WE CANNOT SAY THAT WE ARE THE CHILDREN OF GOD IF WE MURDER OTHER CHILDREN OF GOD. WE CANNOT CLAIM TO BE THE FUTURE BUDDHA IF WE MASSACRE OTHER FUTURE BUDDHAS whether in human form or in animal form. WE CANNOT SAY WE LOVE GOD AND THEN DESTROY HIERS CREATION RELENTLESSLY. AND NOW WE ARE DESTROYING HIERS PLANET. Please teach this again and again to Your trusting followers who look up to You, to Your Holinesses and Reverends as icons of compassion and saintly love. In God's Love, thank You.

Your Reverend Holinesses, Highly Reverend Priests, Priestesses, Monks, Nuns of different faiths, my best wishes and humble prayers for Your wellness in God's mercy. Though my time is tight and precious, as I am still in intensive meditation retreat for World Vegan, World Peace, but the urgent call of the planet and our world push me. I feel I must deliver some urgent messages to Your Holinesses and Reverends. Well, if our house is on fire, we cannot say: "I don't have time to take care of it!" Our planet house is on fire!!! This letter serves the same goal anyway. It's supposed to be sent by post, but I'll read it. It's faster. In time of emergency, too much bureaucracy doesn't help.

Your Holinesses and Reverends... Although the denomination seems varied, but we all serve one God, I believe. We are so grateful, I am so grateful, for the noble, devoted work Your Holinesses and all Your Reverends have been doing over the years, uniting people through spreading the Almighty's message of love and compassion among humans and all of creation. Thank You. May God forever be on Your side.

As great spiritual leaders, You would also be aware of
the devastation occurring on our planet, directly related
to accelerated climate change caused by humans' cruel
behaviors and brutal habits, which is not so difficult to
change once applying the principle of love. Please tell Your
believers this truth. Please keep telling them, please keep
reminding them. I know You did, but we could do more.
Thank You. We just have to change. Tell them that we must
change. We must change if we want to claim that we are
human, that we are the future Buddha, that we are the
children of God! Because WE CANNOT SAY THAT WE ARE
THE CHILDREN OF GOD IF WE MURDER OTHER CHILDREN
OF GOD.

WE CANNOT CLAIM TO BE THE FUTURE BUDDHA IF WE
MASSACRE OTHER FUTURE BUDDHAS whether in human
form or in animal form. As we read the Buddhist Sutras, we
know that even Shakyamuni Buddha repeatedly incarnated
innumerable times as animals. And we know, in the Bible,
God says that Hes even created all kinds of vegetables for
the animals to eat and Hes created many things for us as
well. If the animals mean nothing to God, God wouldn't
have created things for them to eat. Just like God loves us,
so God created things for us to consume. It says that in the

Bible, God created fruit and vegetables in the field and that those shall be our food. (Holy Bible, Genesis 1:29)

WE CANNOT SAY WE LOVE GOD AND THEN DESTROY HIERS CREATION RELENTLESSLY. AND NOW WE ARE DESTROYING HIERS PLANET.

But with over 74 billion land animals alone mercilessly massacred for human consumption every year, the livestock raising industry and its byproducts are responsible for 87% of human-caused greenhouse gas emissions. Not only we are destroying the planet by what we consume, but unspeakable atrocities are happening to innocent animals who have never done anything wrong. Moreover, God created animals to be our friends and helpers, not to be murdered and eaten in such a barbarious way! It is the 21st century, for God's sake.

Love Is The Only Solution

In the Holy Bible, Job 12:7-8, it is said: "But ask the animals, and they will teach you, or ask the birds in the sky, and they will tell you. Or speak to the Earth, and it will teach you, or let the fish in the sea inform you." So, the animals, the Earth that God created are wise, respected beings, whose presence are a great blessing to humans.

But what unpardonable acts against God's Law are we doing to our Heavenly Father's creation? We are destroying God's creatures from land to sea! The abominable cruelty inflicted on God's innocent creatures in lab tests, in livestock raising, in fishing, egg industry, milk, fur, cosmetics, etc., etc... Those industries are undeniably horrific and inhumane. It causes innocent, defenseless, gentle animals, our co-inhabitants, God's creatures, to be imprisoned and tortured, molested in many ways without any chance to defense, or to utter any call for help! Even if they utter some call for help, say the mother cows, the mother pigs were crying when their babies were taken away, beaten, kicked, and murdered, no one would care. Even a five-year-old kid would understand their emotion. It's worse than many hells! Imagine if they are our children, our relatives, our friends or ourselves! They are living beings with emotions, with thoughts, feelings. Any of us who have spent time with a pet, knows that they have their own personalities, they experience love, care, pain and sorrow, happiness and excitement. And loyalty; absolute loyalty. And there is no difference between a house-pet and other animals confined all their life in horrendous concentrated, tight animal factories' crates or fenced-in cramped spaces, rain or shine, no shelter, enduring all kinds of weather, any wicked unimaginable conditions, and whose lives are violently ended at slaughterhouses! For humans' consumption. If we still think that we are human in this case.

For more information, please also watch the following recommended documentaries, such as: award-winning "Cowspiracy," "Earthlings," "Dominion," and award-nominated "What the Health," etc., etc... Also, download free-of-charge "From Crisis to Peace" at Crisis2Peace.org

In all the major religions, there are commonalities, such as the principles: "Do unto others what you would have them do unto you" and "Thou shall not kill." "Ahimsa" meaning nonviolence, etc... Obviously, the eating of any kind of animals, sentient beings is absolutely forbidden in

all main belief systems and holy teachings. Yet too many
of God's children, or religious believers, are not following
these basic guidelines, because we have been led astray by
misconceptions that we need to eat the flesh of animals,
fish, eggs and milk to be healthy. The opposite is true - it has
been proven in scientific and clinical studies that consuming
animals causes innumerable diseases in humans, such as
cancers, all kinds of cancers and heart diseases, thus early
death, and endless sorrow, suffering before that. Not just to
the patients but to their relatives, friends, family members
and loved ones.

It's time now to awaken and change these physically and
spiritually unwholesome, unhealthy, cruel habits, and
the utmost atrocity involved. Our original diet, as per
the Garden of Eden, is the vegan diet. It promotes both
physical and mental and spiritual wellbeing. We can live
happy, healthy lives, thriving purely on plant foods. Actors,
actresses, athletes, sportsmen, martial arts champions,
medical doctors, scientists, Nobel Prize winners, etc…
are glowing proof of a healthy plant-based diet. This
also adheres to "Thou shall not kill," or "Ahimsa," means
no violence, whereas eating animals goes against this

commandment from God. Even if we are not the ones
doing the killing, we cause others to kill for us. The animals
suffer and die just the same, just for our meal, which we
can replace with any other plant-based food. And nowadays
it's even much more so easy. Thus our being, due to
murdering animals, is drenched with blood of the innocent
on our hands. Please teach this again and again to Your
trusting followers who look up to You, to Your Holinesses
and Reverends as icons of compassion and saintly love. So
they would listen to You! WE CANNOT LET SATAN OR MAYA,
THE DEVIL OR THE NEGATIVE FORCE CONTINUE TO LURE
US ASTRAY, AGAINST GOD'S WILL, and against our innate
intelligence and compassionate nature.

Before continuing this letter, I will read a few examples
of the prohibition of animals' flesh eating in the main
world religions. Just in case someone else also is
listening. Someone else who has forgotten the religious
commandments of their own religion. So first I'll read it in
alphabetic order.

THE BAHA'I FAITH

"Regarding the eating of animal flesh and abstinence therefrom, know thou of a certainty that, in the beginning of creation, God determined the food of every living being, and to eat contrary to that determination is not approved."

~ *Selections from the Bahá'í Writings on Some Aspects of Health and Healing*

BUDDHISM

"...ALL MEATS EATEN BY LIVING BEINGS ARE OF THEIR OWN RELATIVES."

~ *Lankavatara Sutra (Tripitaka No. 671)*

"Also, after the birth of the baby, care must be exercised not to kill any animal in order to feed the mother with meaty delicacies and not to assemble many relatives to drink liquor or to eat meat... because at the difficult time of birth there are innumerable evil demons, monsters and goblins who want to consume the smelly blood... by ignorantly and adversely resorting to the killing of animals for consumption... they bring down curses upon themselves, which are detrimental to both the mother and the baby."

~ *Kristigarbha Sutra, Chapter 8*

Another one:

"Be careful during the days immediately after someone's death, not killing or destroying or creating evil karma by worshipping or offering sacrifice to demons and deities... because such killing or slaughtering committed or such worship performed or such sacrifice offered WOULD NOT HAVE EVEN AN IOTA OF FORCE TO BENEFIT THE DEAD, BUT WOULD ENTWINE EVEN MORE SINFUL KARMA INTO PREVIOUS KARMA, MAKING IT EVEN DEEPER AND MORE SERIOUS. ...thus, DELAY HIS REBIRTH TO A GOOD STATE." Or even send them speedily to hell.

~ *Kristigarbha Sutra, Chapter 7*

Karma means retribution. "As you sow, so shall you reap." In the Bible, it states so. "As you sow, so shall you reap." That is the meaning of karma in Sanskrit terms.

Another one:

"If bhiksus do not wear garments made of silk," the silk
that is made from the silkworms, "boots of local leather
and furs, and refrain from consuming milk, cream and
butter therefrom, they will really be liberated... If a man can
control his body and mind and thereby refrains from eating
animal flesh and wearing animal products, I say he will
really be liberated."

Bhiksus means monks.

~ *Surangama Sutra*

Another one:

"If any of my disciples does not honestly consider that and
still eats meat, we should know that he is of the candela's
lineage. HE IS NOT MY DISCIPLE and I am not his teacher.
Therefore, Mahamati, if anyone wishes to be my relative,
HE SHOULD NOT EAT ANY MEAT."

Candela means killer or murderer.

~ *Lankavatara Sutra*

CAO ĐÀI-ISM

"The most important thing is to stop killing... because animals also have souls and understand like humans... IF WE KILL AND EAT THEM, THEN WE OWE THEM A BLOOD DEBT."

~ Teachings of the Saints, About Keeping the Ten Precepts – Abstaining from Killing, Section 2

CHRISTIANITY

"Meats for the belly, and belly for the meats: but God shall destroy both it and them."

~ 1st Corinthians 6:13, Holy Bible

Another one:

"And while the flesh was yet between their teeth, ere (before) it was chewed, the wrath of the LORD was kindled against the people, and the LORD smote the people with a very great plague."

~ Numbers 11:33, Holy Bible

CONFUCIANISM

"All men have a mind which cannot bear to see the sufferings of others.

~ *Mencius, Gong Sun Chou, Chapter 6*

The superior man, having seen the animals alive, cannot bear to see them die; having heard their dying cries, HE CANNOT BEAR TO EAT THEIR FLESH."

~ *Mencius, King Hui of Liang, Chapter 4*

ĐẠO DỪA-ISM

"To have peace, humanity must first have peace with the animals; do not kill them to feed ourselves, then there will be peace among people."

~*Nam Quốc Phật Temple*

ESSENES

"I am come to end the sacrifices and feasts of blood, and if ye cease NOT OFFERING AND EATING OF FLESH AND BLOOD, the wrath of God shall not cease from you."

~ *Gospel of the Holy Twelve*

Love Is The Only Solution

HINDUISM

"Since you cannot bring killed animals back to life, you are responsible for killing them. Therefore you are going to hell; there is no way for your deliverance."

~ Adi-lila, Chapter 17, verses 159-165

Another:

"He who desires to augment his own flesh by eating the flesh of other creatures lives in misery in whatever species he may take his birth."

~ Mahabharata, Anu. 115.47. FS, pg. 90

Another:

"O best of Kings! If the things, acquired by injuring others, be utilized in any auspicious act, they yield contrary results at the time of fruition."

~ Devi Bhagavatam, Fourth Book, Chapter 4, verse 32

ISLAM

"Allah will not give mercy to anyone, except those who give mercy to other creatures."

~ Prophet Muhammad (Peace Be Upon Him), Hadith

Another:

"Do not allow your stomachs to become graveyards of animals!"

~ *Prophet Muhammad (Peace Be Upon Him), Hadith*

JAINISM

"A true monk should NOT ACCEPT SUCH FOOD AND DRINK as has been especially prepared for him INVOLVING THE SLAUGHTER OF LIVING BEINGS."

~ *Sutrakritanga*

JUDAISM

"And whatsoever man there be of the house of Israel, or of the strangers that sojourn among you, that eat anything that has blood*; I WILL EVEN SET MY FACE AGAINST THAT SOUL THAT EATETH BLOOD*, and will cut him off from among his people."

~ *Leviticus 17:10, Holy Bible*
blood: meaning "flesh," which has blood.

SIKHISM

"Those mortals who consume marijuana, flesh and wine - no matter what pilgrimages, fasts and rituals they follow, they will all go to hell."

~ *Guru Granth Sahib, page 1377*

TAOISM

"Do not go into the mountain to catch birds in nets, nor to the water to poison fishes and minnows. Do not butcher the ox."

~ *Tract of the Quiet Way*

TIBETAN BUDDHISM

"The offering to the deities of meat obtained by killing animate beings is like offering a mother the flesh of her own child; and this is a grievous sin."

~ *The Supreme Path of Discipleship: The Precepts of The Gurus, The Thirteen Grievous Sins, Great Guru Gampopa*

ZOROASTRIANISM

"Those plants, I, Ahura Mazda (means God), rain down upon the earth, to bring food to the faithful, and fodder to the beneficent cow."

~ Avesta

etc., and etc. There are more, of course. These are just a few examples.

For further info, please check SupremeMasterTV.com.

So regardless of which faith anyone belongs to, all must keep the most important precept: "Thou shall not kill." Ahimsa. Nonviolence.

Now it's time for humanity to go back to how our Creator originally intended for all Hiers children to live – in dignity, respect, peace, love, and to be good stewards of our Earthly abode. Please remind Your faithful of all this and more. I know You did, but please repeat again and again, and explain to them it's utmost important for their own souls as well as for our planet, for our world. It's time for the suffering of all animals to end, as they have a right to live in peace, freedom and dignity with their loved ones in nature, just as God originally intended.

Please help to rescue God's creation. Please help to end the suffering of innocents. We make war with each other, and we make war with animals. These are not right. These actions are not right. These actions are against God's commandments and will. Please remind Your faithful. I trust in the wisdom of Your Holinesses and all Your Reverends to lead this great change! We must change. I trust that Your Holinesses and Your Reverends, all Your Reverends to lead this great change. To promote the vegan lifestyle, which encompasses love, compassion and respect for all beings and obeys God's commandments. Please promote it to all Your clergy, monks, nuns and all the faithful.

The power of Your entrusted position will lend a significant, effective encouragement for world citizens to follow Your lead. Please be "the hero of our time," rescue all these innocent beings, our fellow co-inhabitants called animals, who have never done any harm. Who are a blessing to our world. Who are wonderful, loving and kind to humans as well as to their own co-inhabitant animals. In our Supreme Master Television, we have ample examples of that, of the animals' loving compassion and kindness recorded from all over the world. Please tell Your faithful to watch them. We

cannot expect Heavens when we create hell or condone
the hellish, massacre of God's beloved creation, in such
a mass-murdering, cold-blooded way. We cannot expect
Heavens' leniency if we destroy God's creation and have
no mercy to other children of God, meaning the animals.

Please do not ignore their horrendous plight. God knows
their daily anguish. Heavens and Earth witness their pain.
Their cries have shaken all Heavens and the hearts of
many beings. Please speak for them, please help them,
as this also helps our world to heal in the wake of climate
acceleration. Your noble deed will be forever recorded by
Heavens and contribute to a benevolent atmosphere on
our planet, to world peace, and to the stabilization of the
climate, which is important to all lives on Earth. All lives
also depend on Your merciful act.

The world citizens, the animals and our children will
forever remember Your heroic, compassionate deeds and
pray for Your happy, prosperous, healthy long life in the
name of God. The ever Merciful Heavens will be pleased.
The all-loving God will pardon our sins and lengthen our
lives, as we pardon and lengthen our co-inhabitants' lives,
the loving, kind animals.

May God bless You, all Your Holinesses and all Your
Reverends, and bless Your holy mission abundantly,
and may God bless our world.

Amen. Thank You. Thank You, and thank You.

In God's Love, thank You.[20]

7
An Urgent Message from
Supreme Master Ching Hai
to All World Leaders and
Governments

*Respected leaders and government officials,
I am really grateful to you for all you have
done up to date, to help our world the best you
can. I thank you all. This is just a reminder,
because I know that you know what's the
right thing to do. You must protect all under
your wings - the co-citizens and the co-
inhabitants, that is, the so-called animals.
They are utterly helpless and à la mercy of
humans' power. The fact is, THERE IS NO
HUMANE SLAUGHTER, no such thing as lawful
murder en masse of the innocents. The WORLD
IS BURNING, threatens to get worse any
moment, HUMANS AND ANIMALS
PERISHING at an alarming rate.*

Heavens and Earth are plaguing us with ever
new, more strange diseases. Destructive signs are
evident everywhere. WARNING SIGNS ARE AMBER
and obvious around our world! Our climate is
accelerating. Animal raising, fish, egg, milk
industries, etc., anything to do with animals,
are the worst producers of lethal methane gas
which heats up our planet. So, stopping these
brutal, murderous businesses is the fastest way
to cool our Earth. You have the power to stop all
this. You have the privilege to IMPLEMENT VEGAN
LAW, NO MORE ANIMAL RELATED SUFFERING
BUSINESSES. Zero pain, agony for all beings,
humans and animals. Because kindness will
beget kindness, and compassion will beget

compassion. Mercy will beget mercy from Heavens. And this VEGAN LAW IS THE MOST EFFECTIVE WAY TO SAVE OUR WORLD. So do not run away anymore from this inevitable decision. Simply just MAKE THE VEGAN LAW AND SIGN IT. Before it's too late for you to decide the right thing, before it's too late to even regret. Before more of God's wrath descends upon us, with more severe weather, more plagues, more terror, more lives lost, more precious resources disappeared, more financial disaster. Work for God, with God. So you will be feeling light, pure and happy by DOING THE RIGHT THING, NOW. Make THE VEGAN LAW to save our world. MAKE VEGANISM THE LAW.

Love Is The Only Solution

This is an open letter to all the leaders and governments of this world. First of all, I want to give you thanks sincerely that you have forsaken privacy, and working irregular hours, long hours to serve the public, and to bring the standard of our co-citizens to a more desirable level in many aspects, while sacrificing personal pleasure, wellness and precious time, plus enduring criticism sometimes. I'm thanking especially the leaders and important ministers, and other high positions in the governments of this world, who try their best to govern the nations with all they have got. I'm helping, by this and invisible ways. I'm supporting you mentally and spiritually. With all love and respect and best wishes, I am sending this letter on air to clarify some of your questions, and maybe some of my not very clear intentions in the letters that I have sent you previously. The most important answer, of course, would be that it's not about how to humanely slaughter, it is about we must NOT SLAUGHTER AT ALL, zero tolerance of animal products.

Respected leaders and government officials, I am really grateful to you for all you have done up to date, to help our world the best you can, especially the higher positions of leadership, such as the kings, the queens, the princes, the princesses, the prime ministers, presidents, ministers

of different departments. I thank you all. In the name of
all citizens of the world, I appreciate what you have done.
It's not easy to be in the leader role and working with so
many different personalities, opinions, and so on. This is
just a reminder, because I know that you know what's the
right thing to do. You know what it is, yes, because you are
smart, that's why you are chosen to lead and help wherever
needed, whomever needed, including our co-citizens, the
animals. But you know what to do. You know deep in your
heart what to do, what's the right thing to do for the world.
Heavens hold you responsible for your work on Earth to
represent justice, to care for God's children. And you know
the cost of not doing it right. You must protect all under
your wings – the co-citizens and the co-inhabitants, that
is, the so-called animals. They are utterly helpless and à
la mercy of humans' power. I wrote many letters to all of
you, all of you who work in the governmental body. Many
of you did answer. Many of you have some questions, all
differently. Some do not answer, maybe because you still
take time to think about this subject. It's heart-wrenching,
isn't it? Because I can hear animals' anguished cries, so how
would you not? You have more protection, for health, etc...
The poor citizens have less – well, many of them poorly can
afford the protection they need. And the animals absolutely

do not have a voice or choice, any lawyers to protect them at all. Pray Heaven have mercy on us and on the animals. Put yourself in their position, so helplessly delivered to brutality. Perhaps you are still pondering about it? We thank Heaven for whatever help rendered to our world and to all beings on this planet. Amen.

Animals, they do have souls, wisdom, knowledge, and even some magical power, visibly and invisibly. Sometimes we can see it, and it's amazing. I'll tell you one of the stories. I live in a kind of remote mountainous area, high in the mountain. There are some monkeys who come to my surrounding, digging some of the roots to eat. And I have given them some food. They always "thank You," thank me. I say, "Thank Heaven. I'm just passing the gift to you. Thank God." And every time they see me, they always greet me with, "We wish You well." "Woo! Woo!" That's "wish You well." And thank you is: "EŔ" Like that. Every time they eat something, because I left it outside, and I cannot always wait for them to eat, so I'm inside. And even they have finished the food, they wait. The king of the monkeys waits for me to pop out or somewhere in the window and say the "EŔ!" before he left. The stories about the animals who have helped me or show their intelligence are a lot, it's just

we don't have a lot of time
to tell everything here. Just
maybe one more story of
the spider who saved my
life. The spider. This spider
was very big, bigger than
the size of my palm. Almost
the size of my stretched-
out palm. One night,
about two o'clock in the
morning, I was meditating

and suddenly I got up. I wanted to write something in my
diary and then I saw a big spider and it's the second time
he came to warn me about something. So, I said, "What is
it today?" He told me, "Don't turn off the light. Stay away
from the sofa." And I was thinking, "Why is that?" And then
I saw a snake crawling, almost reached where I was sitting.
So of course, I used a net kind of instrument, people use
it to catch the butterfly or something from the house to
bring them out. So, I used that to let him crawl in and I
put him outside. I was really grateful that he saved my life
that day because it was a very poisonous snake, I can tell
by the color and the triangle shape of his head. And the
story of the monkeys is much longer but I don't want to

tell too much about animal stuff because the letter is long. I probably will tell it to my so-called disciples at another time. And also, the story about the squirrels, etc., etc. So many stories about animals who showed me their intelligence and goodness. Actually, I asked the spider, "Why are you so good to me? That's the second time you've helped me." The spider told me that, "Oh, because You are very kindhearted. You have never killed us." I said, "Kill you? How would I even think about that." He said, "Not just the spider type but You save all the insects from Your house. You never killed any of us insects. So, we also have to help You." That's what he said.

Animals, they are wonderful. It is unfortunate for us that we do not preserve our telepathy communication, which is universal and very convenient for all beings to communicate with each other without language. Because we have so many languages, and animals, they also have their own languages, so it would have been more convenient for us if we could remember how to communicate inside. And animals, even trees, they helped me many times, so I'm very, very indebted to them. Just recently, because I am making so many speeches concerning peace for the world and peace for the animals, so of course, whatever leftover from the negative subordinates, they disturb me a lot, making all kinds of trouble. If cannot directly to me, then they make trouble to my assistants, etc., or make something happen. Just to waste my time, to disturb my concentration from my intensified meditation retreat.

I am still in retreat, but God told me I have to write this to you. And I don't have enough time to keep writing to each of you all the time like I did. So I will send this on air. Perhaps it's more convenient for all of you to listen, because it's all only one answer: the VEGAN DIET, the VEGAN WORLD, that will rescue our planet and secure lasting peace for all beings on Earth. I guess you know already what to do, I do hope. I do see some very little, tiny baby steps toward the benevolent world of veganism. Well, at least many nations are helping other less fortunate nations and some needy people around the world, and I'm very, very grateful for that. Thank God and bless you. Our world has become better, that's for sure. BUT NOW WE HAVE ONE MORE STEP TO GO: THE VEGAN STEP. Then all will be perfect, you will see. All will be peaceful. Everyone will relax, happy. Happier than now, more peace than now. It could be paradise too.

But you're still thinking about it, about what to do to have a vegan law, to tell everyone to be vegan, and do away with

all meat, eggs, milks, fish. When I say meat, I mean fish also
and whatever that moves. And even eggs are no good for
us, also involved a lot of killing. And raising animals of any
kind is making our planet climate change worsen because of
the methane and all kinds of economical-related problems.
You are thinking hard. Maybe that's why you try also very
hard to avoid the most lethal enemy of our world. The one
that causes the degradation of our human status, causes
death, by the billions, of humans and animals; maims,
disables other billions of lives and continues to do so every
day!!! But there's no time to think now. Please, DO ACT
QUICKLY. We MUST STOP ALL THIS. We are a civilized race of
beings, intelligent race of beings. It's the 21st century. Many
Masters come and go, teach us benevolence and kindness
to all beings. We cannot continue massacring other beings
or humans. You have the power to stop all this. You have
the privilege to IMPLEMENT VEGAN LAW, NO MORE
ANIMAL RELATED SUFFERING BUSINESSES. Zero pain, agony
for all beings, humans and animals. And ANIMAL LAWS IS
THE BEST. ANIMAL PROTECTION LAW, meaning VEGAN LAW,
no more causing any harm, any pain, any fear to animals.
Because kindness will beget kindness, and compassion will
beget compassion. Mercy will beget mercy from Heavens.
"As you sow, so shall you reap." The Bible states that. All the

main religions of the world state that. And this VEGAN LAW
IS THE MOST EFFECTIVE WAY TO SAVE OUR WORLD.

Because you know well by now, by the UN's warning, by
scientific research reports, you know, we know that the
meat, fish, eggs, milk, laboratory tests on animals, leather
industry; ANYTHING TO DO WITH HURTING ANIMALS,
domestic or wild, ARE DETRIMENTAL TO OUR WORLD. We
talk about all kinds of climate reduction, or reducing air
pollution BUT animal raising, fish, egg, milk industries, etc.,
anything to do with animals, are the worst producers of
lethal methane gas which heats up our planet. So, stopping
these brutal, murderous businesses is the fastest way to
cool our Earth.

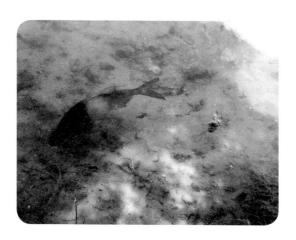

By the way, whales, you know, the big giant gentle "fishes" in the sea, they are savers of our world, savers of oxygen. They keep CO2 in them for a long, long time, and they produce at least 50% atmospheric oxygen for our world. Imagine that? And still some people are hunting them, for food! Making excuses such as scientific research. What do we have to do any research with the fish who has existed, I mean, hundreds of thousands of years in the sea? If we don't touch them, we leave them alone, God takes care of them. There is a report. I'll read it to you, from Dr. [Ralph] Chami, Dr. Thomas Cosimano, Dr. Connel Fullenkamp and Sena Oztosun that we aired on our recent Noteworthy News, on Supreme Master Television, December 28, 2019. For your reference, here it is: "International Monetary Fund report calls for urgent conservation of whales to address climate change" – even! How wise. "Economists from the United States analyzed research about whales' role in capturing carbon. Described in IMF's 'Finance & Development' publication, they explained that a whale can sequester an estimated 33 tons of carbon during his or her lifetime, while in comparison, a tree absorbs up to 22 kilograms per year. The carbon is stored in the whale's body and stays out of the atmosphere for hundreds of years, even after he or she passes away." It stays within her body

and stays out of our atmosphere. Can you imagine that?
So God has arranged many savers, angels in disguise, in
the form of the animals, to help us. Naturally, the whales
stay in the ocean, if she passes away naturally in the ocean,
then she stays there. "In addition, the whales' life activities
promote the growth of phytoplankton." Repeat: "The
whales produce phytoplankton, which provides at least 50%
of atmospheric oxygen and captures 40% of global carbon
annually." Forty percent. The whales capture 40% of global
carbon annually. Imagine. Wow. During their lifetime. All
the whales, are like that. And that is their mission. I repeat:
"The whales capture 40% of global carbon annually." The
whales. Here is the website for you to review. Oh, I will put
it on the screen for you to read. OK?

https://www.imf.org/external/pubs/ft/fandd/2019/12/
natures-solution-to-climate-change-chami.htm

Our climate is accelerating, our world is in danger. But
you seem to still go around forever in a circle, maybe still
thinking of what to do. You mention anything, but not the
center target. We target many other areas but not the
center point. Just like scratching outside of the thick socks
does not relieve the itch. By now, scientists have warned
us XXXXX times, many times, repeatedly, by evidence –

that vegan is the best, most effective way to reduce global warming, reducing or stopping climate change, stabilizing it, is good for all of us, human and animal tenants. Yes, we are just tenants of this world house. No right to damage it without being fined heavily.

I am just scripting this down as words come to my mind without much order. I beg your pardon. My anguished heart doesn't make it easy for me to be flowery or beat around the bush. God is dictating my hand as prayers surge within my heart for a WORLD-VEGAN, so that we will have lasting WORLD PEACE for all on Earth! Please pray to God and do your part. You can, you have the power to lead world citizens into the right way of life, pleasing Heavens and Earth and all that live. We are all grown up, honest citizens, God-fearing, law-respecting. So there's no need to be flatteringly fake. I respect you, your intelligence, so I will not tell you anything less than honesty and truth. Plus, we are all transparent in the eyes of Heavens, and every day so much untold suffering all around our world, that's witnessed by Heaven and Earth.

We all know that meat eating is the No. 1 killer in our world. But it seems to me that mostly, some governments are trying so mightily to cover this by aiming at or diverting attention to any other subjects or activities that have very much less or zero effect. We should ask ourselves if we want to be on humane's side, God's side or the killer's side??? Please answer yourselves and act on it now. Act on God's benevolent side, or we will go down in history as murderers... Because the consequence is graver than any wars and killing up to date combined. You know that because you are intelligent. You know that because you are smart. Yes! You must be smart to act or be selected as leaders. In some Asian countries, the leaders and governments are called "parents of the people." In case I offend you, I sincerely apologize but still have to do it, because we are all in danger of extinction; animals and humans, have to speak out because the WORLD IS BURNING, threatens to get worse any moment, HUMANS AND ANIMALS PERISHING at an alarming rate. Heavens and Earth are plaguing us with ever new, more strange diseases. Destructive signs are evident everywhere. WARNING SIGNS ARE AMBER and obvious around our world!

Someone has to speak up more loudly. I have to speak up more loudly. All the governments signed the less meat protocol, but haven't done anything concrete for it. Oh!

Love Is The Only Solution

God help our world! But maybe God doesn't want to hear us anymore. Hes might have turned Hiers head from our prayers, because your hands are full of innocent blood. I quote the Bible that many of you know. That is Isaiah Chapter 1:15. God doesn't want to hear our prayers if we do not change our way of life and wash our hands of the sins we have committed by murdering en masse other living beings. Why is it that we do things against God's will? Why is it that we do things against our own conscience? Against any logic and reason of an intelligent race? We are supposed to be "the Crown of Creation," the children of God, the future Buddhas.

On one hand, we say that we make the law to protect animals from harm, from maltreatment or pain or fear of any kind. But on the other hand, just brutally murder them outright en masse, and given soo much, so much unspeakable torturing before their death. SO THIS IS A CONTRADICTION THAT I DO NOT UNDERSTAND. Or maybe you think that squeezing them in a tight space, chaining them, drowning them in disinfectant tanks, cutting their throats alive, etc... are acts of benevolence and protection? Are they acts of benevolence and protection? And those are justified laws, really? The fact is, THERE IS NO HUMANE

SLAUGHTER, no such thing as lawful murder en masse of the innocents. They harm us in no way. They don't commit any crime. That's unjust. That's not justice. Please think about that and be thinking quick. So we have to do the opposite. Please DECLARE VEGAN LAW, NOW. NO MORE ANIMALS- SUFFERING PRODUCTS of any kind. It's so simple, it's so simple. Just put down that piece of bloody dripping meat, everyone, from now, from whatever living beings that meat or product might have come from. We just ban them all. MAKE THE VEGAN LAW AND SIGN IT. Prohibit all animal suffering procedures, forbid all of them if we are to redeem ourselves and rescue our planet. God will bless us more. Hes already said, "Hes doesn't want any animal sacrifices even for Hirmself," as stated in the Bible. "Don't bring me any more sacrifices. Don't bring me any more animal sacrifices." Yes. It's said somewhere else also in the Bible. "When you lift your hands in prayer, I will not look. Though you offer many prayers, I will not listen, for your hands are covered with the blood of the innocent victims." They are victims.

I'm wearing this white band. It's an Asian tradition. It's a sign of mourning. Please mourn with me. Please pray for all the innocent, anguished souls that have suffered since

countless eons, countless thousands of years in the hands
of humans, war and slaughter for food, etc., and pray for
their deliverance. Pray for their freedom from anguish,
sorrow, hatred. Let them go rest in high Heavens. If God
doesn't want any animal sacrifices for Hirmself, how would
Hes want us to even kill them and eat their bloody flesh?
So do not run away anymore from this inevitable decision.
Nowadays, we have so much tasty vegan food everywhere.
Healthy, happy for all, humans and others. The sooner we
make this decision to make Vegan Law, the better for our
conscience, for all of us here on the planet; so that we can
also be spared of judgement. So act by your loving inherent
nature. Oh, my kind human fellow beings, God granted you
the power to take care of our world. What are you doing
with it? Please act on it now and rescue our world. Simply
just MAKE THE VEGAN LAW AND SIGN IT. Before it's too
late for you to decide the right thing, before it's too late to
even regret. Before more of God's wrath descends upon
us, with more severe weather, more plagues, more terror,
more lives lost, more precious resources disappeared,
more financial disaster. King David of old killed only one
person wrongly, yet his citizens got punished with a plague
for three days. In our time, we have like forever plagues,
one after another, where can we escape?

Fatal Epidemics / Pandemics Originally Transmitted by
Eating Animals

HIV / AIDS – transmitted by chimpanzees

Variant Creutzfeldt-Jakob Disease (Mad Cow Disease) –
transmitted by cows

H5N1 Avian (Bird) Flu – transmitted by chickens, geese

SARS (Severe Acute Respiratory Syndrome) – transmitted
by civets

H1N1 Swine Flu (Pig's Disease) – transmitted by pigs

MERS (Middle East Respiratory Syndrome) – transmitted by
camels

Ebola – transmitted by bats

COVID-19 – transmitted from bats to pangolins

All these diseases are transmitted FROM ANIMALS TO
HUMANS

Where else can we move to? We have only one planet.
Plus, vicious wild fires, typhoons, earthquakes, tsunamis
etc… relentlessly. Heavens and Earth are shaken to the core,

seeing the atrocities we measure upon our fellow human and animal Earth tenants. So, all kinds of calamity are inevitable. By the latest plague Wuhan, the mass death toll is still rising, millions of people, are quarantined. Though the number of deaths and quarantined are minimized by some governments, fearing to alarm the public, fearing its effect on the economy! I'm sure you all know. Please open your eyes, please open your minds, open your heart, see the reality around you. Use your privileged position of power that God bestowed upon you to make it right for our world. You are put in these high positions to take care of everyone on this planet, to make it right, to be a good steward on Earth. So please don't waste your time and God's blessing anymore. Do it now, change it now, not thinking any longer before things get more out of control. Before disaster might befall us suddenly and we have no time to react. My prayers are with you, our loving fellows' prayers are with you. Work for God, with God. You will be stronger, happier and feel more relieved, in body, mind and soul, of the burden of guilt in your heart, that will fall away. So you will be feeling light, pure and happy by DOING THE RIGHT THING, NOW. Make THE VEGAN LAW to save our world. MAKE VEGANISM THE LAW.

God doesn't want any suffering for any beings. Not any
blood, any flesh of animals or any other beings. Not even
the circumcisions. What for? What good does it do to God
to make poor helpless babies suffer and die? Just a few
days old and have to suffer and die in uncounted numbers
ever since this practice begun, because of related after-
effects. Bleeding or infection. Imagine the sorrow of the
parents. Imagine how God feels? We make God suffer also.
Because God made us in Hiers own image. We are God's
children. When the children suffer, God suffers. God said
to me, it was not Hiers wish at all. It was Satan the devil
who faked Hiers name to harm the pure-hearted, the
vulnerable faithful. To trap them into more suffering, to
kill more of the heirs, the male heirs, who can make their
country strong, make people multiply, and prosper. Think
about it, what kind of God would like to inflict pain on poor
innocent, helpless babies and children or even male adults,
for what? What for God wants to cause worry and pain for
their parents. They are also Hiers children. Even my heart,
even they are not my children, I'm not their parents, but my
heart was in soo deep anguished feeling for their sorrow
and pain, especially for the unfortunate helpless babies,
how would the All-Loving God be able to bear it, not to say
Hes even ordered that!? In the name of God, the utmost

just and merciful, I beg forgiveness from all countless innocent beings tormented and massacred by humans since time immemorial. Intentionally or unintentionally. Now it's the 21st century we must be more civilized. We must stop superstitious violent tradition. We must stop harming innocent babies and animals and humans. It is Satan the devil that initiates anything that makes beings suffer. That's his hell style. He is Hell, of course, a symbol of suffering, sorrow, pain, anguish and anything that is no good, that is negative, that is dark and causes pain. So please save your innocent babies and children. I will tell you why the devil wants the male babies, or male children, or males to suffer. I will tell you why.

God told me this, it was not the merciful God. It's the zealous demons, Satan's subordinates. They like to eat the flesh of anyone who dies in war and conflict and agony, and the like. Recently, I cannot bear no more, they also bother me too much. So, 80% of these demons are already dragged into hell recently by the Original Universe Godses Protectors. Because these kinds of demons, they might not be Satan himself but they work for Satan, and they try to always incite hatred between humans, and between humans and animals, or between animals, between all beings, to enjoy their inflamed energy. They live off it, and they enjoy their anguish, dead flesh as well. They told me. The zealous demons (or spirits) even told me not to make peace on Earth because then they will not have anything to eat. I say, "I cannot grant your wish. You can only follow me, go home, go to Heaven. That's all I can promise you. I cannot continue to let people or animals suffer on this planet. Enough. Too much already!" They said they cannot eat anything else. I ask them, "Cannot you just eat, naturally dead animals or other corpse, like abandoned corpse or something?" They said, no they cannot because it's a different energy. They need to eat the kind of flesh that has anguish, hatred, sorrow or fearful, terrorized kind of flesh of beings who have inhabited dead corpses because every other flesh has different energy, they cannot eat. I said, "Well, you have to change, I cannot continue to let you make war just so that you can eat something." They said even just a small piece of flesh from this kind of anguished, terrorized energy flesh, they can be satisfied for a long time. I said, "No matter what I cannot condone this request, I cannot condone this practice. I love humans, I love animals. All the souls are innocent until they're trapped onto this planet by chance. I'm not going to let them suffer anymore. So the best is that you follow me, go

home." Some did, but very little (small number). Actually up to today, 82% of these demons are already dragged to hell. I had an excuse to do that, because they bother me.

Please save your precious children. You can see there is no use to make them suffer and even die, in many cases. In America it is reported that there are at least 100 babies die every year, due to related after-effects of the circumcision. The number could be more but some parents don't report. You can understand why. They are just too anguished even to think of reporting or they don't even want to talk about it. But look at the history and you can see nothing good came out of worshipping such a sadistic sort of "god." It cannot be God. God is love. God is caring, loving, compassionate, merciful. Hes created children, Hes created man in Hiers own image. How would Hes want Hiers children to suffer? It's not logical. You are smart, you understand. So look back. Look around, nothing good came out of worshipping such sadistic sort of demons. Just endless war, mass suffering, perishing of innocent children and babies in big numbers. And even some decades ago. You remember, you know that. You know the holocaust. Please stop it. Please stop torturing your babies and children, or and yourself, or and your friends. Wake up.

Wake up, wake up. There is no such God that makes your babies suffer. Your babies are precious to you and God knows that. God doesn't want to torture you mentally, physically or your babies. For what? Hes knows the consequences, well at least it's very painful. If we cut a little bit of our finger, we feel it's so painful already. How would a baby bear it? How would the babies be able to bear it? I'm sorry if I have offended you in any way but my heart is... I feel like it's boiling. I feel... I feel... I feel like something is boiling. Thinking of these babies, and imagining how they have to feel so helplessly delivered. Just babies, a few days old, my God. PLEASE STOP IT! Otherwise God will punish you more. Devils, only the devils, they want to weaken your nation, cannot you see that? Because baby males or male children or male adults are our future, especially baby children (I cannot read) especially male baby, and male children, they are future Rabbis, they're future presidents, they're future defenders of your country. So the devils want to hurt them, kill them. So that your countries are weakened. Less males to help to strengthen the nation and do many works for the society, for your country. Can you see that? I'm telling you the truth. For what reason I do this? Risking myself, to offend you? Devils they are everywhere. They can manifest themselves as humans,

they will look dignified and tell you that they are god or they are saints.

Remember the story of Solomon. He has been in exile for three years and the demons took over his throne and his household, his country and he made so many disgusting, cruel deeds and people thought that it was Solomon but it wasn't. Solomon was exiled all three years, until he came back. And the devils driven away. And Jesus, when He was meditating in the desert, also the devil came and tempted Him. He promised, he bribed Him with the whole world as a gift, if Jesus but just bowed to Satan. So what did Jesus say? "Get thee behind Me," meaning get lost! The Buddha also did the same thing when devils came to tempt Him. But in his vulnerable state of mind and in his very innocent faith, someone might have heard it wrong, or the translation was wrong? Thinking it's God's voice. So, thus God sent Messengers to correct, to clear Hiers name, to clear Hiers order, which was not Hiers order, so other Messengers came saying that Hes doesn't want any animal flesh, even animal flesh and blood, how would Hes even want to harm the children? Hes loves animals so much Hes doesn't want them to suffer, how would Hes want your children, your babies to suffer, even risking death. Think about it, OK?

The mistranslation has cost millions or billions of lives of the innocents. For example, in India, in the old times, in the Rigveda 10.18.7, it's stated that widow women whose husbands are deceased, are advised to go ahead in their lives. The word agre means "go ahead." However, agre was mistranslated and misinterpreted as agne, meaning fire. And thus, the hymn became: "Let these wives first step into the pyre, tearless without any affliction and well adorned." So, "go ahead," instead of "go in the fire." They were completely different definitions. Many women were forced to die in the pyre, the fire that burns the dead. If her husband is dead and they burn him, she has to be burnt with him. So, many women in the old times were forced to burn with their husbands in the fire, rather than moving forward in their lives, as the word agre means. So this is terrible. And also in Atharvaveda 18.3.1, it's one of the most quoted Vedic mantras, which supports a woman to be burned with her husband when he's dead: "Choosing her husband's world, O man, this woman lays herself down beside the lifeless body. Preserving faithfully the ancient custom. Bestow upon here both wealth and offspring." The misinterpretation arises from "choosing her husband's world," which has been understood as the wife being advised to join the dead husband in the afterlife, in the next

world. So, she must burn herself in the funeral pyre of her husband. Since 1829, this practice of burning alive a widow with her husband was outlawed in India. But still it occurs on some rare occasions as it is regarded by some Hindus as the ultimate form of womanly devotion and sacrifice.

So you see, mistranslation can kill and kill terribly, and kill the innocents. We have to be careful about what we believe and what we follow, because we have to listen to logic, intelligent reason, if we want to follow the will of God. Just for an example, because here is a contradictory statement in the same Veda. Atharvaveda 18.3.2, it is stated that: "Rise, come unto the world of life, O woman: come, he is lifeless by whose side thou liest." So this mantra indicates that the woman should rise from beside the dead body of her husband and move on with this living world. Also, in the Vedas, it is spoken of widow remarriage. So, wrong interpretation can kill many, many innocents. That's what I meant by, it could be that people heard wrong or translated wrong. Please, save your babies, save your children, save your male people. Let them live. Let them be whole and healthy and well. God has created them perfect. We cannot molest it or lessen any part of his body. That will be against God's will.

So, for your own sake, common sense, morality, reputation and honor, please do the only right thing now to PASS THE VEGAN LAW. NO MORE KILLING OF THE INNOCENTS, ANIMALS OR MEN. And by the way, all the citizens on this planet, please support your government to pass the VEGAN LAW so animals don't have to suffer any more. Please protect your children. God doesn't want to hurt them. God wants to love, to protect them, so they can grow up to be good rabbis, to be good priests, good monks, good presidents, good leaders, or the strong working force for your country, for your family. That is the real God. The God I know is like that. All forgiving. If you just repent, you will be forgiven. I promise that, with whatever honor I have. Please believe me. God is all loving, all forgiving. Just turn around, do the right thing. Repent. God will be forgiving you, 100%. That is the real God, very caring for your wellness, making Heavens to wait for you. There cannot be a God who wants to eat animal flesh and drink animal blood and harming babies and children. Especially men, whom any nation or family rely on for their strength, for their protection, for anything that needs power and heroism and idealism. So we cannot harm any male babies or male children, any males. We need them. There are also other customs or wicked traditions somewhere that even molest females,

similar situation. Circumcise the female organs and make them suffer, bleeding, infected and death also. Mostly done without anesthesia. Can you imagine? Can you imagine you are under that situation? Helplessly delivered to anguished pain like that.

Stop all this. You wise governments, you have power, stop all this barbarous superstition. You have enough education and you have enough power to stop all this. Otherwise God will not forgive us, not forever. God cannot be patient forever seeing us harming other fellow co-inhabitants. But if we stop, we repent, God will immediately forgive and forget and we will all enjoy this life in abundance, happiness, and go to Heaven when we leave this world. I promise. Heavens are my witness, God is my witness. The planet may survive, the world might make it but those who ignore their conscience or and live off the suffering of other innocent beings, such as animal slaughtering, they will not be spared of judgment. So act by your loving-hearted inherent nature. Governments of the world and citizens of the world, work together in unison to make our world a happy place to live. To leave behind a better planet for our children. May God still be with you. May God bless your VEGAN LAW decision. Be courageous, be heroic, righteous, virtuous, fearless in God's mission and protection. All of you, leaders, governments and co-citizens of the world, please, stop killing the innocent animals, babies or man. Heavens will help you. Do the VEGAN LAW, DO SIGN IT and do follow through with it. THAT'S THE RIGHT THING to do for all the governments, all the leaders and all the citizens in this world. That's the only priority right now if our world is to survive and well, and IF WE WANT TO AVOID THE PUNISHMENT OF HELLFIRE. I thank all of you. The beings in this world thank all of you. Again, just DO THE RIGHT THING. DO THE VEGAN LAW, DO SIGN IT. Do practice it, do follow through. Do be vegan. THAT'S THE RIGHT THING and that's all you have to do. Everything else will fall into place. It will be all benevolence, merciful, compassion, happiness all over our planet if you do that. With all my love, best wishes and God bless. Thank you again. You understood it all. Please just do it. Just one act of righteousness, VEGAN LAW and VEGAN LIFESTYLE. Thank you. May God still bless our world. May God still be with us all.[21]

8 Words of Encouragement from Master

Because vegan diet brings a holy and protective atmosphere, a loving atmosphere into our planet, into our surroundings, and that energy will protect us. This is something maybe we cannot prove, but it's very logical. Whatever we do affects us. So, being vegan, meaning compassion for animals, and bear in mind already that we want to save the planet by being vegan, that means very compassionate because we want to save the planet.

How many billions of trillions of beings on this planet including man and animal? Therefore, if we have this idea in our head, we are very compassionate and being that compassionate the energy around you is great and very, very benevolent to all that surrounds you. And if everyone on the planet had such a benevolent energy surrounding them, then the planet became Heaven again. And it's not only saved, it will become much better than now; more beautiful, more abundant and everything, every wish will come true.

My goodness, I wish everybody understands what I'm talking about. Thank you. You see, energy is something we cannot prove, but we can feel it. For example,

suppose you have a loving partner with you, who day in day out together, and one day you argue. That day, even though you don't talk to each other or you don't throw books at each other, you feel terrible, because the energy in the house is not peaceful, is not loving, is not harmonious and cooperative.

So that is the thing about energy, although we cannot prove it. Maybe we could, scientists have discovered many things about human energy. When somebody is angry, they can feel the energy going in a low direction, and when you are happy, they can measure the energy, more benevolent and more beneficial.

So, the energy that we create by loving animals and by wanting to save the planet is immense, and it's going to affect you and everyone around it. So, logically speaking, vegan diet is the protection that we need. We need this protective energy.[22]

Have big love. Big, big, big! The bigger the better. Love all that you see around you.

We have nothing to lose. Just replace that piece of animal's dead carcass instead with tasty healthy plant-made protein of all types. Be vegan, make peace. That's all we have to do, and love. Love as much as you want, just don't make war. Thank you so much. God bless us all.[2]

We are compassion. We are merciful, we are caring. So, we just have been cheated. We have been misinformed up to now, so we did not know it. Being vegan worldwide is the advancement of compassion that will uplift and unify all cultures, bringing tranquility to humans and animals alike.

The inner peace that comes from replacing killing with respect for all life will spread like a wave across the globe, elevate human hearts, and create a harmonious Eden on Earth. That will bring us all to a lasting Golden Era.[19]

Love Is The Only Solution

Our nature is love and compassion, as the Buddha has taught us. We have been misled life after life by our own ignorance, and the darkness of this realm has imposed pressure upon us that we forget even more. So, never have I blamed humans for forgetting to love themselves, the animals, or forgetting what they really are—that is, love.

Humans are love incarnate. But it is time to remember again, or else we face extinction by our own hands. One way to start to love animals is to understand what they experience. Go watch a slaughterhouse, go watch a killing of a goat, a horse or a sheep, or chicken, a pig, or watch it on television or a video, to know the true horror, fear, anguish that is behind the nicely packaged piece of flesh. If a person knows the truth about the hellish terror that these animals feel, it would be hard to swallow that piece of their flesh.

You ask, how can we improve our loving quality? I call it LQ. Humans, we have many Q's: IQ, LQ,

GQ (God Quality) also. Animals and humans both have this Loving Quality (LQ), and fortunately, humans are more privileged because we can improve our Loving Quality in exercising the love, like a muscle. So without changing our normal schedule at all, we can just flex and develop our love muscles at breakfast, lunch, and dinner; no need exercise.

Be veg to show love, as well, to your family, your pets, your friends, and your enemies, and extend this love to all the world's co-inhabitants at large. Even to the trees, the plants, the flowers, the stones, the pebbles. Just being vegan alone, automatically after a few days or a few weeks, you'll feel something change in you. Your own loving nature will flow effortlessly like a spring, spring of love. You will be more able to receive the love and blessing from the sun, the moon, the stars, from all of nature and our co-inhabitants. And the animals will suddenly, truly, look like friends and neighbors – so beautiful, friendly, intelligent and loving.

Then it's very easy for you to love them, and extremely difficult to ever dream of harming them again, even indirectly, or consuming their suffering flesh.[23]

9 Pray for World Vegan

We pray together. Even if you can't be vegan now, just pray to be soon. Pray for world vegan. **Please join us every day from 9 to 10 pm, Hong Kong Time, to pray or and meditate for World Vegan**, thus we will also have lasting World Peace. May Heaven's bless you multifold. Thank you so much.

Our prayers are powerful because it's backed by Heavens and Saints and God Power. It has tremendous power, never before known, especially now we do it together, and you became vegan, praying to be vegan, going to be vegan, with all your benevolent quality within. It's very effective. Please tell your family members, friends, acquaintances, whomever you know to pray with us for a vegan world. It's good for them also. We pray, meditate together about an hour, continue every day again until World Vegan is here.

Even sincere for five minutes, twenty minutes, that all helps to clean up our world, to save our children and to live a noble, worthy, decent life, befitting the children of God. Join us to rescue the innocents. Join us to rescue our world. Please! May God bless you multifold, in this life and the next.

**Make an alarm wherever you are,
whatever you do, please stop for some
moments to pray for World Vegan with us,
9 to 10 pm, Hong Kong time.**[24]

References

Preface

1. Supreme Master Ching Hai on the Environment:
    A Noble Goal & Change of Heart Can Save the Planet,
    videoconference with Association members in Au Lac
    (Vietnam) on July 20, 2008. Video 839.

    http://video.godsdirectcontact.net/daily/2008.09.26/
    BMD743.wmv

2. "The Real Love" – A Musical that Unites Hearts,
    teleconference in California, USA on August 27,
    2011. DVD 999.
    suprememastertv.com/en1/v/136665388570.html

Chapter 1

3. Wake Up and Be Vegan in This Time of Cleaning,
    conference with Supreme Master Television team
    on June 26, 2020.
    suprememastertv.com/en1/v/102385733924.html

4. Wake Up and Be Vegan in This Time of Cleaning,
    conference with Supreme Master Television team
    on June 26, 2020.
    suprememastertv.com/en1/v/102057990937.html

Chapter 2

5. Humanity's Leap into the Golden Era, international
    conference in Washington DC, USA on November 8,
    2009.
    suprememastertv.com/en1/v/131957486562.html

Chapter 3

6. To Love God Is to Keep Hiers Commandments,
   in Panama on November 29, 1989. Video 106.

   http://www.suprememastertv.tv/bbs/board.php?bo_
   table=download&wr_id=8423&goto_url=&sfl=wr_content&st
   x=To+Keep+Hiers+Commandments&sst=wr_num&sop=and&
   url=link2&year=&month=&day=

   The Key of Immediate Enlightenment Book 3, pp 104-106.
   http://www.smchbooks.com/ebook/data/english/E-The%20
   Key-E3.pdf

7. Global Unity: Together in Saving Lives, international
   conference in Hong Kong on October 3, 2009.
   Video 882-1.

   http://video.godsdirectcontact.net/daily/2009.11.22/
   WOW1165.wmv

8. Be a Torchbearer for God, public lecture in Johannesburg,
   South Africa on November 25, 1999. Video 667.

   suprememastertv.com/en1/v/99665258964.html

Chapter 4

9. Interview with Supreme Master Ching Hai by The Irish Dog
   Journal on December 16, 2009. Video 899.

   http://video.godsdirectcontact.net/daily/2010.03.24/
   WOW1287.wmv

10. Children's Health and Sustainable Planet,
    international conference in Jeju Island, South Korea
    on September 21, 2009. Video 881-3.

    http://video.godsdirectcontact.net/daily/2009.11.10/
    WOW1153.wmv

11. Leading a Virtuous Lifestyle in Accord with the Law of Love, videoconference with Association members in Los Angeles, USA on July 31, 2008. Video 842.

    http://video.godsdirectcontact.net/download/2008.10.31/Between_Master_and_Disciples_2008.10.31_778.wmv

12. Through Selfless Action We Can Attain Fulfillment, group meditation in Singapore on March 7, 1993. Video 326.

13. Media Interviews with Supreme Master Ching Hai :
    James Bean of Spiritual Awakening Radio,
    Bob Lebensold of Environmentally Sound Radio,
    Ms. Andrea Bonnie of Irish Independent Newspaper in United States & Ireland on July 29,
    September 11 & November 21, 2008. Video 854-1.

    http://video.godsdirectcontact.net/download/2008.09.28/Words_of_Wisdom_2008.09.28_745.wmv

14. World Vegan Brings Lasting World Peace, videoconference with Supreme Master Television team on December 24, 2020.
    suprememastertv.com/en1/v/118282097128.html

Chapter 5

15. The Return of the King.
    suprememastertv.com/en1/v/126653410185.html

    Let Peace Begins with Us, public lecture in Malaysia on October 1, 1989. Video 99.

16. Bless Yourself with Meditation: Selections from the book of "Coloring Our Lives" by Supreme Master Ching Hai.
    suprememastertv.com/en1/v/129254659480.html

17. Meditation Is Your Shield, conference with Supreme Master Television team on September 02, 2020. suprememastertv.com/en1/v/111118523935.html

18. The Quan Yin Method- Meditation on Inner Light and Inner Sound. suprememastertv.com/en1/meditation

19. Humanity's Leap into the Golden Era, international conference in Washington DC, USA on November 8, 2009. Video 818-2.

    suprememastertv.com/en1/v/132161236579.html

Chapter 6

20. Supreme Master Ching Hai's Appeal to All Religious and Spiritual Leaders, video message on March 2, 2020. suprememastertv.com/en1/v/88425789933.html

Chapter 7

21. Supreme Master Ching Hai's URGENT Message to All World Leaders and Governments, video message on March 24, 2020. suprememastertv.com/en1/v/90753335579.html

Chapter 8

22. Celestial Art, English edition international book premiere in Los Angeles, USA on December 12, 2008. Video 852-2.

    http://video.suprememastertv.com/daily/2009.01.14/ WOW853.wmv

23. The Love of Centuries, Mongolian edition international book premiere in Ulaanbaatar, Mongolia on April 22, 2011. Video 950-1

    http://video.suprememastertv.com/daily/2011.06.01/WOW1721.wmv

Chapter 9

24. Supreme Master Ching Hai's Urgent Call to Pray for World Vegan in Order to Rescue Our World, video message on February 6, 2020. suprememastertv.com/en1/v/85783840493.html

Author: The Supreme Master Ching Hai

Published by: Love Ocean Creative International Company
P.O. Box 109-973 TAIPEI, TAIPEI CITY,
11099 Taiwan (R.O.C)
Tel: 886-2-87896317
E-mail: service@loveoceancreative.com

http://www.smchbooks.com

First Edition: September 2021
Second Printing: November 2021
ISBN: 978-0-578-98254-0 (paperback)

For more information please visit
www.SupremeMasterTV.com